Money Saving Secrets

"Money-Saving Secrets Only the Rich Know!"

Copyright © 2024 JWH Jr.

Money Saving Secrets

Legal Notice:- *This book is for informational purposes only. Any slights of people or organizations are unintentional and the Development of this book is bona fide. In no event will the author and/or marketer be liable for any direct, indirect, incidental, consequential or other loss or damage arising out of the use of this document by any person, regardless of whether or not informed of the possibility of damages in advance.This book has been distributed with the understanding that we are not engaged in rendering technical, legal, accounting or other professional advice.*

Money Saving Secrets

Table of Contents

Book Introduction..8
Chapter 1: The Mindset Shift: Thinking Like the
Wealthy...12
    Introduction to Wealthy Mindset........................12
    Understanding Money as a Tool...........................13
    The Importance of Financial Goals.......................13
    The Power of Education..14
    Embracing a Long-Term Perspective......................15
    Overcoming Limiting Beliefs................................16
    Practicing Gratitude..16
    Conclusion..17
Chapter 2: Budgeting Mastery: Building a Rich Path 18
    The Importance of Budgeting..............................18
    Understanding Your Income and Expenses............18
    The 50/30/20 Rule..19
    Creating Your Budget..20
    Tracking Your Spending......................................21
    Adjusting Your Budget..22
    Automating Savings..22
    Conclusion..23
Chapter 3: Investing 101: Where the Rich Put Their
Money...23
    Understanding Investing.....................................24

Copyright © 2024 JWH Jr.

    Types of Investments..24
    Building Your Investment Portfolio........................26
    The Power of Compound Interest............................28
    Seeking Professional Advice.....................................28
    Conclusion...29

Chapter 4: Credit Scores: The Hidden Wealth Tool...30
    What is a Credit Score?...30
    How is Your Credit Score Calculated?....................30
    Why Credit Matters...32
    How to Improve Your Credit Score..........................32
    Monitoring Your Credit..34
    Conclusion...34

Chapter 5: Tax Strategies: Let Uncle Sam Work for You..35
    Understanding Taxes..35
    The Basics of Taxation...35
    Tax Strategies for Savings...36
    Staying Informed and Seeking Help.......................38
    Conclusion...39

Chapter 6: Smart Shopping: Quality Over Quantity..39
    The Philosophy of Smart Shopping........................39
    Assessing Needs vs. Wants..40
    The "Cost Per Use" Mindset......................................41
    Smart Shopping Strategies.......................................41
    The Value of Experiences Over Items....................43

Money Saving Secrets

Conclusion..43
Chapter 7: The Power of Networking: Financial Friends..44
   Networking as a Wealth Builder........................44
   Why Networking Matters.....................................45
   Strategies for Effective Networking.....................45
   Building Genuine Relationships..........................47
   Finding Mentorship...47
   Conclusion...48
Chapter 8: Savings Apps and Tools: Digital Solutions for Wealth...49
   The Rise of Financial Technology........................49
   Why Use Savings Apps?.....................................49
   Top Savings Apps...50
   Investment Apps...52
   Safety and Security...53
   Conclusion...53
Chapter 9: Real Estate: The Gateway to Wealth........53
   The Allure of Real Estate Investing.....................53
   Why Invest in Real Estate?.................................54
   Types of Real Estate Investments........................55
   Getting Started in Real Estate.............................56
   Managing Your Real Estate Investments...............58
   Conclusion...58

Copyright © 2024 JWH Jr.

Chapter 10: The Art of Negotiation: Get the Deal You Deserve..................59
   The Importance of Negotiation Skills....................59
   Understanding the Basics of Negotiation..............59
   Preparing for Negotiation......................................60
   Strategies for Effective Negotiation.....................61
   Negotiating Salary..62
   Conclusion..63

Chapter 11: Health is Wealth: Investing in Your Future 64
   The Link Between Health and Wealth...................64
   The Cost of Poor Health.......................................64
   Investing in Your Health.......................................65
   The Financial Benefits of Good Health.................66
   Conclusion..67

Chapter 12: Lifestyle Choices: Spending Less to Live More..................68
   The Connection Between Lifestyle Choices and Wealth..................68
   Minimalism: The Power of Less...........................68
   Practicing Mindful Spending................................70
   Cutting Costs Without Sacrificing Quality.............71
   Conclusion..71

Chapter 13: The Importance of Financial Literacy: Knowledge is Key..................72
   Understanding Financial Literacy........................72

The Building Blocks of Financial Literacy..............73
Resources for Financial Education........................74
Embracing Continuous Learning..........................75
Conclusion..76
Chapter 14: Side Hustles: Creating Additional Income Streams...76
The Rise of the Side Hustle....................................77
Why Consider a Side Hustle?................................77
Finding the Right Side Hustle................................78
Balancing Time and Energy...................................79
Success Stories...80
Conclusion...80
Chapter 15: Future Planning: Building Wealth for Generations...81
The Importance of Future Planning.......................81
Setting Long-Term Goals.......................................82
Building an Emergency Fund.................................83
Investing for the Future..83
Regularly Reassess Your Financial Strategies........84
The Power of Generosity.......................................85
Conclusion...85
Final Thoughts..86

Introduction

In a world where financial education is often overlooked and the complexities of wealth can seem daunting, it's crucial to understand that saving money is not just a habit—it's a mindset. **"Money-Saving Secrets Only the Rich Know!"** reveals the financial habits and strategies that affluent individuals employ to build and maintain their wealth. This book is designed to demystify the secrets of the rich and provide practical tips that anyone can implement to improve their financial well-being.

Have you ever wondered how some people seem to effortlessly glide through life with financial security, while others struggle to make ends meet? The truth is, the wealthy see money through a different lens. They don't just earn money—they manage, invest, and save it in a way that enables them to multiply their resources over time. This book will explore these practices, helping you not only to save more but to think like the rich.

We'll start by shifting your mindset. To change your financial realities, you must first change how you view your relationship with money. The wealthy tend to see money as a tool for achieving their goals, whether that involves starting a business, investing in real estate, or saving for retirement. They know that the more knowledge they have about their finances, the better decisions they can make. This book will teach you how to adopt this mindset.

Next, we will dive into practical strategies for budgeting. This isn't about choosing between your morning coffee and saving for your vacation; it's about creating a plan that allows you to enjoy your life now while securing your financial future. You'll learn how to set a budget that works, how to allocate your funds effectively, and how to track your expenses without feeling stifled by the process.

Investing is another essential area we will explore. Many people think of investing as a game reserved for the elite, but the truth is that understanding the basics of investing can change your financial landscape. We'll demystify the world of stocks, bonds, and real estate, giving you the confidence to explore these avenues on your own.

Equally important are the less obvious aspects of money management, like maintaining a healthy credit score, smart shopping techniques, and leveraging tax strategies. These are the tools that can multiply your savings, lessen your expenses, and create a robust financial future.

You'll also discover the power of networking and understanding how the rich use their connections to enhance their financial growth. Building relationships with like-minded individuals can open up new opportunities for collaboration, investment, and mentorship.

Throughout this book, you'll find practical tips and actionable advice, ensuring that every chapter offers takeaways you can apply immediately. We will discuss the significance of having multiple income streams and how even the smallest side hustle can lead to significant financial gain over time.

Lastly, planning for the future is crucial. We will talk about the importance of creating a savings plan, understanding long-term investments, and preparing for unforeseen circumstances. Building wealth isn't just about the present; it's also about securing a legacy for your family.

In **"Money-Saving Secrets Only the Rich Know!"** you will find wisdom, encouragement, and most importantly, a blueprint for taking control of your finances. It's time to stop letting money dictate your life and start mastering it. Welcome to the first step in your journey to financial freedom.

Chapter 1: The Mindset Shift: Thinking Like the Wealthy

Introduction to Wealthy Mindset

The first step on the journey to financial freedom involves transforming your mindset. Many people think that wealth is a result of luck or privilege. However, it's often the case that the well-off cultivate specific habits and thought processes that enable them to thrive financially. In this chapter, we'll dissect what it truly means to think like the wealthy and how anyone, regardless of their current financial status, can adopt this mindset for themselves.

Understanding Money as a Tool

The wealthy tend to view money as a tool for creating opportunity. This perspective is essential. Rather than seeing experience or money as something that dictates their happiness or success, they view it as a means to an end. Ask yourself: How do I view money? Is it a source of stress, or do I see it as a resource I can leverage?

To shift your mindset, try reframing your thoughts. Suppose you receive a paycheck. Instead of thinking, "I can spend this on bills," think, "I will use this to invest in my future." This simple change in perspective can lead to a significant shift in how you budget and save.

The Importance of Financial Goals

To think like the wealthy, you must set clear financial goals. Wealthy individuals typically have a vision for their financial future, which acts as a roadmap for their spending and saving habits. Consider what your long-term goals are: Do you want to buy a home? Start a business? Retire early? Write them down. This clarity will guide your decisions and motivate you to achieve those targets. Wealthy people often break their long-term goals into smaller, manageable milestones. Achieving these smaller goals provides a sense of accomplishment that motivates them to keep moving forward.

The Power of Education

Wealth is often not just about having money but about knowledge. The wealthy continuously educate themselves on finance, investments, and market trends. They read books, attend seminars, and seek mentorship to further enhance their knowledge. Start incorporating learning into your daily routine. Whether it's reading a finance-related book, listening to a podcast, or following financial experts on social media, becoming financially literate is essential for cultivating a wealthy mindset. Additionally, consider investing in courses that expand your financial knowledge. These don't always mean formal education; many online platforms offer affordable or even free resources. The key is to stay curious and never stop learning.

Embracing a Long-Term Perspective

While many people focus on immediate gratification and short-term pleasure, the wealthy take a long-term view of their financial health. Instead of living paycheck to paycheck, they prioritize saving and investing for the future.

To develop a long-term perspective, create a savings plan. Set aside a portion of your income for future investments or savings. This practice not only helps secure your financial future but also instills discipline in your spending. Think of it as a "pay yourself first" strategy; make your savings a non-negotiable part of your budget.

Overcoming Limiting Beliefs

Everyone has limiting beliefs that can hinder their financial success. These beliefs often stem from societal norms or personal experiences about money. Common examples include thoughts like "I'll never be wealthy," or "money is the root of all evil." To adopt a wealthy mindset, it's crucial to recognize and challenge these beliefs. Start by identifying any negative beliefs you have about money. Write them down and analyze them. Ask yourself if they are rooted in fact or simply fears. Replace those negative beliefs with positive affirmations. For example, if you catch yourself thinking "I will never be able to save," counter it with "I am capable of building my savings."

Practicing Gratitude

Finally, wealthy individuals often express gratitude for what they have, which can lead to a more positive outlook and better financial choices. Take time daily to appreciate what you have. It could be your job, the money you've saved, or relationships that add value to your life. Gratitude shifts your focus away from what you lack and instead highlights what you can build upon.

Conclusion

Changing your money mindset doesn't happen overnight, but the effort is worth it. By viewing money as a tool, setting financial goals, continuously educating yourself, embracing a long-term perspective, overcoming limiting beliefs, and practicing gratitude, you'll be aligning your thoughts with those of the wealthy. This alignment will pave the way for better financial decisions and ultimately, create a positive trajectory for your savings and investments.

Chapter 2: Budgeting Mastery: Building a Rich Path

The Importance of Budgeting

Budgeting is often considered a dull and oppressive task, but in reality, it's one of the most powerful tools you can use to gain control over your financial life. For the wealthy, budgeting is not about deprivation; it's about planning and prioritization. In this chapter, we'll explore how to create a budget that not only helps you save money but also allows you to enjoy life along the way.

Understanding Your Income and Expenses

The first step in mastering budgeting is understanding your income and expenses. Take a moment to list all your sources of income—this might include your salary, freelance work, rental income, or investment returns. Now, let's move on to expenses. Make a comprehensive list of your monthly expenses, including fixed costs like rent or mortgage payments, utilities, groceries, insurance, and variable costs like entertainment, dining out, and shopping.

Once you have this information, you can see how much money you have coming in versus what's going out. If your expenses exceed your income, it's a wake-up call to make adjustments.

The 50/30/20 Rule

One effective budgeting method adopted by many wealthy individuals is the 50/30/20 rule. This simple guideline helps you allocate your income effectively, ensuring you're saving while also enjoying your life.

1. **50% for Needs:** This category includes all your essential expenses—housing, food, transportation, and basic necessary bills.

2. **30% for Wants:** This is where you can allocate money for fun activities, hobbies, and lifestyle choices like entertainment, dining out, or vacations.

3. **20% for Savings and Debt Repayment:** This portion focuses on your future. Use it to build your savings, invest, and pay down any debt.

By following this structure, you're ensuring a balanced approach to spending and saving. It allows you to live within your means while preparing for your financial future.

Creating Your Budget

With an understanding of income, expenses, and the 50/30/20 rule, it's time to create a budget. You can use a simple spreadsheet, budgeting apps, or even pen and paper. Here's how to get started:

1. **Calculate Your Monthly Income:** Add up all sources of income to form a total.

2. **List Your Expenses:** Create a detailed list of your monthly expenses, categorized into needs, wants, and savings/debt repayment.

3. **Compare:** Subtract your total expenses from your income. If you have money left over, great! Consider increasing your savings or paying off

debt. If you are over budget, identify areas to cut back.

Tracking Your Spending

Once your budget is made, the next step is to track your spending. It's easy to lose sight of your financial goals when money is flowing in and out. This is where budgeting apps can come in handy. They help monitor your transactions and categorize your spending, providing insights into your habits.

Adjusting Your Budget

One of the key aspects of effective budgeting is flexibility. Life is unpredictable, and your budget may need to be adjusted periodically. If you find that you consistently overspend in certain areas, reevaluate those budget categories.

Don't be afraid to experiment with different allocations until you find what works best for you. Building and maintaining wealth takes time, and adaptability is crucial.

Automating Savings

To truly master budgeting, consider automating your savings. Set up automatic transfers from your checking account into savings or investment accounts. This process ensures that you're saving consistently without having to think about it. Out of sight, out of mind is the motto here—save first and spend what's left.

Conclusion

Budgeting is not merely a tool for the wealthy; it is the foundation of financial mastery. By using strategies like the 50/30/20 rule, tracking your expenses, and automating savings, you can create a path that leads to wealth. Remember, the goal of budgeting is not just to restrict you but to empower you to make informed financial decisions that align with your long-term dreams.

Chapter 3: Investing 101: Where the Rich Put Their Money

Understanding Investing

Investing is a term that often intimidates those not familiar with the concepts, but it doesn't have to be. Investing is simply about putting your money to work so you can earn more money over time. Wealthy individuals understand the importance of making their money grow, and they have diverse portfolios to mitigate risks.

Types of Investments

There are several types of investments that you can consider. Let's break down some of the most common options:

1. **Stocks:** Stocks represent shares of ownership in a company. When you buy a stock, you are essentially buying a small part of that company. Stocks can provide significant returns, but they do come with risk due to market fluctuations.

2. **Bonds:** Bonds are essentially loans that you give to a company or government. In return, they promise to pay you interest over a specified period and return the principal at maturity. Bonds are considered safer than stocks but usually offer lower returns.

3. **Mutual Funds and ETFs:** These are investment vehicles that pool money from multiple investors to purchase a diversified portfolio of stocks, bonds, or

other securities. They offer a lower-risk option, since diversification can help reduce the impact of a poor-performing asset.

4. **Real Estate:** Investing in real estate involves buying property to rent out or sell for profit. Real estate can provide a consistent income stream and tends to appreciate over time.

5. **Cryptocurrency:** A newer but increasingly popular investment type, cryptocurrencies like Bitcoin and Ethereum are digital assets that can be highly volatile. Therefore, thorough research and caution are necessary here.

6. **Retirement Accounts (401(k)s, IRAs):** These accounts offer tax advantages for retirement savings. Contributing to these accounts can be

one of the best investment decisions you make.

Building Your Investment Portfolio

A key principle of investing is diversification. This means spreading your investments across various asset classes to reduce risk. A well-balanced portfolio might include a mix of stocks, bonds, real estate, and mutual funds.

To build your own investment portfolio, follow these steps:

1. **Determine Your Risk Tolerance:** Everyone has a different level of comfort with risk. Knowing how much risk you can tolerate will help steer your investment choices.

2. **Set Your Investment Goals:** Think about what you want to achieve. Are you investing for retirement, a major purchase, or simply to build wealth?

Your goals will influence your investment strategy.

3. **Choose an Investment Strategy:** This could be a hands-on approach, where you personally select and manage your investments, or a hands-off approach, using index funds or robo-advisors that automatically balance your portfolio.

4. **Regularly Reassess Your Portfolio:** Your financial situation, goals, and risk tolerance may change over time. Regularly reassess your investments and make adjustments as necessary.

The Power of Compound Interest

One of the most profound concepts in investing is compound interest, often referred to as "interest on interest." The earlier— and more consistently— you invest, the more you can benefit from this exponential growth.

Consider this: If you invest $1,000 at an annual return of 5%, after 30 years, you'll have around $4,321 without adding any additional contributions. This power of compounding illustrates why starting early is so important.

Seeking Professional Advice

While it's important to educate yourself, don't hesitate to seek professional advice. Financial advisors can help customize your investment strategy based on your individual goals and risk tolerance. However, ensure that any advisor you work with is fiduciary, meaning they are legally obligated to act in your best interest.

Conclusion

Investing is a critical component of wealth-building, but it is essential to educate yourself before diving in. By understanding the different types of investments, fostering a diversified portfolio, leveraging compound interest, and potentially working with a financial advisor, you, too, can make your money work for you. Remember, the wealthy don't just work for money; they ensure that their money works for them.

Chapter 4: Credit Scores: The Hidden Wealth Tool

What is a Credit Score?

A credit score is a three-digit number that reflects your creditworthiness. It influences various aspects of your financial life, including your ability to secure loans, interest rates, and even rental applications. For the wealthy, maintaining a favorable credit score is a priority since it opens up opportunities for better financial products and services.

How is Your Credit Score Calculated?

Understanding how credit scores are calculated can help you improve or maintain yours. The key components of a credit score typically include:

1. **Payment History (35%):** This is the most significant factor. It measures whether you pay your bills on time and any missed payments can significantly impact your score.

2. **Credit Utilization (30%):** This is the ratio of your current credit card balances to your credit limits. It's best to keep this under 30% to be viewed positively.

3. **Length of Credit History (15%):** The longer you've had credit accounts

open, the better it reflects on your score. Older accounts help establish a solid credit history.

4. **Types of Credit (10%):** Having various types of credit (credit cards, loans, mortgages) can enhance your score, showing that you can manage different kinds of debt responsibly.

5. **New Credit Inquiries (10%):** Opening several new accounts in a short time can be viewed negatively. Limiting hard inquiries can help maintain your score.

Why Credit Matters

A good credit score can save you money by qualifying you for lower interest rates on loans and mortgages. For instance, if you're taking out a mortgage, a lower interest rate can mean thousands of dollars in savings over the life of the loan.

Additionally, some employers check credit scores as part of their hiring process, especially in financial roles, so a positive score can enhance job prospects.

How to Improve Your Credit Score

Improving your credit score doesn't happen overnight, but consistent effort can lead to excellent results. Here are some strategies to boost your score:

1. **Pay Bills on Time:** Set reminders or automate payments to avoid late fees that can hurt your score.

2. **Reduce Debt:** Focus on paying down existing debts to lower your credit utilization ratio. This may involve consolidating debts or prioritizing high-interest items first.

3. **Check Your Credit Report:** Review your credit report annually for errors or inaccuracies. Dispute any issues you

find, as corrections can improve your score quickly.

4. **Don't Close Old Accounts:** Keep older accounts open, even if you don't use them often. They contribute positively to your credit history.

5. **Be Strategic About New Credit:** Limit the number of new credit applications and keep hard inquiries to a minimum.

Monitoring Your Credit

Many financial institutions offer free credit monitoring services. Utilize these tools to keep track of your credit score and stay informed about any changes. Knowing where you stand allows you to take proactive steps if your score dips.

Conclusion

Your credit score can be a powerful tool in building and maintaining wealth. By understanding what affects your score and taking proactive measures to improve it, you can unlock better financial opportunities and save money in the process. Just like budgeting and investing, managing your credit score is an essential piece of your financial puzzle.

Chapter 5: Tax Strategies: Let Uncle Sam Work for You

Understanding Taxes

Taxes can be quite the burden, but understanding how they work and using effective strategies can significantly influence your financial situation. Wealthy individuals often take advantage of available tax benefits and deductions, allowing them to maximize their income and savings.

The Basics of Taxation

Taxation can seem complex at first, but let's break it down. Most people pay federal income taxes, and depending on where you live, you may also pay state and local taxes. The more you earn, the higher your percentage in taxes can be due to a progressive tax system.

Understanding the different types of taxes is crucial:

1. **Income Tax:** This is a tax on your earnings, typically taken out of your paycheck.

2. **Capital Gains Tax:** This tax applies to the profit made from selling investments. Long-term capital gains (assets held for over a year) are usually taxed at a lower rate than short-term gains.

3. **Property Tax:** Homeowners often pay property taxes based on the value of their property.
4. **Sales Tax:** This is added to purchases. The rate varies by state or locality.

Tax Strategies for Savings

By employing specific tax strategies, you can reduce your taxable income and save money. Let's explore a few effective methods:

1. **Maximize Deductions:** Deductions reduce your taxable income. Keep track of eligible expenses, including mortgage interest, charitable donations, medical expenses, and business expenses if you're self-employed.
2. **Contribute to Retirement Accounts:** Contributing to accounts like a 401(k) or IRA can lower your taxable income.

These accounts grow tax-deferred, meaning you won't pay taxes until you withdraw funds in retirement.

3. **Utilize Health Savings Accounts (HSAs):** If you have a high-deductible health plan, consider contributing to an HSA. Contributions are tax-deductible, and withdrawals for qualified medical expenses are tax-free.

4. **Invest Tax-Efficiently:** Investments held in taxable accounts can create tax liabilities due to capital gains. Consider holding stocks for over a year to benefit from lower long-term rates and taking advantage of tax-deferred accounts for other investments.

5. **Consider Tax Credits:** Unlike deductions, tax credits directly reduce your tax bill. Research available credits such as the Earned Income Tax Credit (EITC) or education credits, which can

substantially lower the amount you owe.

Staying Informed and Seeking Help

Tax laws can change frequently, so staying informed about updates is essential. Various resources like IRS publications, tax books, and IRS webinars can provide guidance.

Additionally, consider hiring a tax professional, especially for more complex situations. A skilled tax advisor can help you navigate the rules and optimize your tax strategy.

Conclusion

Understanding tax strategies is crucial for wealth accumulation. By maximizing deductions, contributing to retirement accounts, investing wisely, and staying informed, you can take control of your tax situation and minimize the burden. Tax efficiency not only keeps more money in your pocket but also helps you build financial security over time.

Chapter 6: Smart Shopping: Quality Over Quantity

The Philosophy of Smart Shopping

When it comes to shopping, the wealthy have mastered the art of prioritizing quality over quantity. Instead of impulsively buying on a whim, they make thoughtful decisions that ensure they get the best value for their money. This chapter will explore how you can adopt a similar approach to your shopping habits.

Assessing Needs vs. Wants

The first step in smart shopping is discerning between needs and wants. Needs are essentials, like food, shelter, and transportation, while wants are items that enhance your lifestyle but are not necessary. Start by listing your purchases in both categories.

When tempted to buy something, ask yourself: "Is this a need, or just a want?" Developing this habit can lead to more conscious spending.

The "Cost Per Use" Mindset

When considering a purchase, think about the **cost per use**. This concept encourages you to evaluate how often you will use an item and what that equates to in terms of cost.

For instance, consider the purchase of a quality winter coat versus a cheap one. If the expensive coat lasts for ten years versus the cheaper one lasting only two, you're essentially paying more per wear for the cheaper version. Evaluating items this way can shift your perspective toward investing in quality.

Smart Shopping Strategies

1. **Create a Shopping List:** Before heading out—or when shopping online—create a list based on your needs to avoid impulse buys. Stick to the list!

2. **Research Before Buying:** Don't rush into purchases. Take your time to research products and compare prices from different retailers. Websites like PriceGrabber or apps like Honey can help you find the best deals.

3. **Look for Quality Investments:** For significant purchases like furniture or appliances, focus on quality and longevity. Investing in better-quality items can save money in the long run as you won't need replacements or repairs as often.

4. **Use Coupons and Discounts:** Be on the lookout for coupons, promotional codes, or seasonal discounts. However, ensure it's an item you genuinely need rather than purchasing something just because it's on sale.

5. **Buy Used or Refurbished:** Many high-quality products, like electronics or furniture, can be found second-hand or refurbished at a lower price while still delivering excellent value. Check sites like Craigslist, Facebook Marketplace, or certified refurbished sections on manufacturers' websites.

The Value of Experiences Over Items

Wealthy individuals often prioritize spending on experiences rather than material goods. Research shows that spending on travel, meals, or activities often brings more long-lasting happiness than buying possessions.

Consider allocating a portion of your budget to experiences that create memories rather than accumulating material goods. This mindset change can lead to more fulfilling purchases.

Conclusion

Smart shopping is about making informed, conscious decisions that prioritize quality and long-term value. By assessing your needs, embracing the cost per use approach, using research, and focusing on experiences, you can transform how you shop—ultimately enhancing your financial well-being while also enriching your life.

Chapter 7: The Power of Networking: Financial Friends

Networking as a Wealth Builder

Networking isn't just about exchanging business cards; it's about building relationships with individuals who can influence your financial future. Wealthy individuals understand the significance of surrounding themselves with like-minded, driven individuals, and you can do the same.

Why Networking Matters

Building a network of contacts can open doors for collaboration, investment opportunities, and wealth-building strategies. Those who have a strong network often find job opportunities, mentorship, and financial advice more easily.

Additionally, relationships can lead to partnerships or joint ventures, allowing you to tap into new markets or enhance your business acumen.

Strategies for Effective Networking

1. **Identify Your Goals:** Clarify your purpose for networking. Are you looking for potential business partners, mentors, or investors? Understanding your goals will help you choose the right events and connections to pursue.

2. **Attend Networking Events:** Look for community events, workshops, or seminars related to your interests. Meetup.com, Eventbrite, and industry-specific conferences are excellent places to begin.

3. **Engage in Online Networking:** Social media platforms, especially LinkedIn, can be powerful tools for connecting with professionals in your field. Join industry groups and participate in discussions to showcase your expertise.

4. **Leverage Your Existing Network:** Don't forget about your current contacts. Inform friends, family, and colleagues of your goals, as they may have valuable connections or advice to share.

5. **Follow Up:** After meeting someone, send a follow-up message expressing pleasure in meeting them. Follow-up keeps the connection alive and opens doors for future discussion.

Building Genuine Relationships

Focus on building genuine relationships rather than merely trying to get something from people. Offer value to your network by sharing knowledge, providing assistance, or connecting them with others.

A genuine approach fosters trust and can lead to mutually beneficial partnerships that can be financially rewarding in the long term.

Finding Mentorship

Mentorship can be invaluable in your financial journey. Seek mentors who have achieved what you aim to accomplish. They can provide guidance, insights, and encouragement—helping you avoid common pitfalls and fast-track your success.

When approaching a potential mentor, be clear about what you're hoping to gain and how you appreciate their expertise. Show genuine interest in their work to create a solid connection.

Conclusion

Networking can significantly influence your wealth-building journey. By identifying your goals, actively participating in networking opportunities, and fostering genuine relationships, you can establish a powerful network that enhances your financial opportunities. Remember, you don't always need to connect with established individuals; even strong connections with peers can lead to future opportunities. Embrace the power of social connections, and watch as new doors open in your financial journey.

Chapter 8: Savings Apps and Tools: Digital Solutions for Wealth

The Rise of Financial Technology

In today's digital age, technology plays a pivotal role in managing finances. Savings apps and financial tools can simplify budgeting, investing, and tracking progress toward your financial goals. This chapter will explore some of the top savings apps and tools available to help you on your wealth-building journey.

Why Use Savings Apps?

Savings apps offer numerous advantages:

1. **Convenience:** Most savings apps can be accessed from your smartphone, making it easy to track your savings, investments, and spending on the go.
2. **Automation:** Many apps allow you to automate savings, ensuring you consistently put money aside without thinking about it.
3. **Insights:** Financial tools can provide valuable insights into your spending habits, helping you make informed decisions.

Top Savings Apps

1. **Acorns:** This app rounds up your purchases to the nearest dollar and invests the spare change automatically. It's an excellent way to start investing without actively thinking about it.

2. **Digit:** Digit analyzes your spending habits and automatically sets aside money for savings without any effort on your part. This makes saving effortless, as you'll hardly notice the small withdrawals.

3. **Qapital:** Qapital allows you to set savings goals and create rules for saving, such as saving a certain amount when you make a purchase or when you reach specific spending limits.

4. **YNAB (You Need a Budget):** This budgeting tool helps you allocate every dollar of your income and gives insights into where your money goes.

Its proactive approach to budgeting promotes financial discipline.

5. **Mint:** Mint is a comprehensive budgeting app that tracks all your accounts in one place. It categorizes your spending, tracks your bills, and provides insights on where you can save.

Investment Apps

Investing doesn't have to be reserved for the wealthy. Several apps make it accessible for everyone:

1. **Robinhood:** Known for its commission-free trading, Robinhood allows you to buy and sell stocks without fees, making it an attractive option for beginners.

2. **Stash:** This app allows you to start investing with as little as $5 and teaches you about the stock market

along the way. You can select personalized investment options based on your interests.

3. **Betterment:** Betterment is a robo-advisor that manages your investments based on your financial goals, helping you create a diversified portfolio without direct management.

Safety and Security

When using financial apps, it's essential to prioritize safety and security. Look for apps that use encryption, secure transactions, and have positive reviews regarding customer service and security features.

Conclusion

Savings and investment apps are valuable tools in your wealth-building arsenal. From budgeting to investing, these platforms provide insights and automation that help you make informed financial decisions and consistently save money. Embrace technology, and leverage these digital solutions to empower your financial future.

Chapter 9: Real Estate: The Gateway to Wealth

The Allure of Real Estate Investing

Many wealthy individuals have built substantial wealth through real estate investing. Properties can appreciate over time, provide passive income, and offer significant tax advantages. In this chapter, we'll explore why real estate is a valuable investment and how you can get started.

Why Invest in Real Estate?

1. **Appreciation:** Real estate tends to appreciate over time, meaning the value of your property can increase.

Though market conditions can fluctuate, long-term trends often show overall growth.

2. **Cash Flow:** Rental properties offer a stream of passive income through rental payments. This cash flow can cover your mortgage and other expenses while providing profit.

3. **Tax Benefits:** Real estate investors may benefit from deductions such as depreciation, mortgage interest, and repair costs, lowering their overall tax burden.

4. **Leverage:** Real estate allows for leverage, meaning you can borrow less than the total value of the property. For example, if you purchase a $200,000 property with a $40,000 down payment, you can reap the benefits while only putting in a fraction of the price.

Types of Real Estate Investments

1. **Residential Real Estate:** This includes single-family homes, apartment buildings, or condo units purchased for rental income. Many beginning investors start here.

2. **Commercial Real Estate:** These properties—such as office buildings, retail spaces, or warehouses—tend to have longer leases and provide potentially higher returns, but they also require more capital and expertise.

3. **Real Estate Investment Trusts (REITs):** If direct property ownership isn't appealing, consider investing in REITs, which allow you to invest in real estate portfolios that pay dividends.

Getting Started in Real Estate

1. **Education:** Before investing, educate yourself on the property market, financing options, and local regulations. Various books, websites, and courses can provide insights.

2. **Networking:** Build relationships with professionals in the industry, such as real estate agents, property managers, and fellow investors. They can provide valuable knowledge and support.

3. **Analyze Properties:** Look at potential properties and analyze their cash flow, expenses, and market conditions. Seek properties that meet your investment goals.

4. **Secure Financing:** Determine how you'll finance your purchase. This may include conventional loans, FHA loans, or private lenders. Understand the implications of each option regarding terms and interest rates.

5. **Conduct Due Diligence:** Once you find a property, perform thorough inspections and assess the neighborhood. Being diligent in this stage can save you from costly mistakes.

Managing Your Real Estate Investments

If you decide to manage rental properties yourself, be prepared for the responsibilities involved, such as tenant screening, maintenance, and bookkeeping. Alternatively, consider hiring a property management company to handle these tasks.

Conclusion

Real estate has long been a pathway to wealth for those willing to educate themselves and commit time and resources to it. By understanding the benefits of real estate investing, exploring various investment types, and taking calculated steps to get started, you can add this powerful asset to your wealth-building strategy.

Chapter 10: The Art of Negotiation: Get the Deal You Deserve

The Importance of Negotiation Skills

Negotiation is a skill that many successful individuals possess. Whether you're negotiating a salary, making a purchase, or discussing a contract, understanding how to negotiate effectively can lead to more favorable outcomes. In this chapter, we'll explore negotiation strategies and techniques to empower you in financial discussions.

Understanding the Basics of Negotiation

At its core, negotiation is about reaching a mutually beneficial agreement. It's a communication process involving offer and counteroffer. Becoming a skilled negotiator can save you money, increase your income, and enhance your satisfaction in various aspects of life.

Preparing for Negotiation

Preparation is critical in negotiation. Before entering any discussion, consider the following steps:

1. **Know Your Goals:** Clearly define what you want to achieve. Establish a minimum outcome you can accept while aiming higher to leave room for concessions.

2. **Do Your Research:** Gather information regarding the topic of

negotiation—whether it's a job offer or the price of a car. Knowledge about industry standards or competing offers can strengthen your position.

3. **Understand the Other Party:** Consider the perspective of the other party. Understanding their goals and limitations can help you create mutually agreeable solutions.

Strategies for Effective Negotiation

1. **Practice Active Listening:** Listening is as crucial as speaking in negotiation. By actively listening to the other party, you can respond appropriately and demonstrate that you value their input.

2. **Stay Calm and Confident:** Maintaining composure and confidence during negotiations helps convey that you mean business. Keep your body language assertive but open.

3. **Create Win-Win Solutions:** Aim to find solutions that satisfy both parties. If you can identify common ground, it makes the negotiation process smoother and fosters a positive relationship.

4. **Be Willing to Walk Away:** Know your limits. If the terms are unfavorable, don't be afraid to walk away. This tactic can sometimes lead the other party to reconsider their offer.

5. **Practice Patience:** Rushing a negotiation can lead to hasty agreements. Allow for pauses to think, gather your thoughts, and create an opportunity for the other party to reconsider their positions.

Negotiating Salary

When negotiating a salary, keep the following tips in mind:

1. **Research Average Salaries:** Know the average salary for your position in your industry and location. Websites like Glassdoor or Payscale provide valuable insights.

2. **Consider the Whole Package:** Salary is only one part of your compensation. Benefits, bonuses, and opportunities for advancement can also hold significant value.

3. **Practice Your Pitch:** Role-playing potential conversations with a friend can help you gain comfort and clarity in expressing your expectations and justifying your requests.

Conclusion

Negotiation is an invaluable skill that can enhance your financial life significantly. By preparing thoroughly, practicing active listening, maintaining confidence, and seeking win-win outcomes, you can achieve favorable agreements in many areas of your life—ultimately contributing to your overall wealth and well-being.

Chapter 11: Health is Wealth: Investing in Your Future

The Link Between Health and Wealth

When discussing wealth, we often focus on finances, investments, and assets. However, health is the ultimate asset that lays the foundation for financial success. Healthy individuals can perform better at work, are generally happier, and can save money on healthcare costs. In this chapter, we'll explore the connection between health and financial well-being and how to invest in your health.

The Cost of Poor Health

Poor health can lead to significant financial burdens, including medical bills, lost wages, and decreased productivity. Chronic illnesses can drain savings and lead to stressful situations, making it increasingly difficult to build wealth.

Conversely, maintaining good health enhances job performance, which can lead to promotions, raises, and better opportunities.

Investing in Your Health

To ensure you're in the best shape to pursue your financial goals, consider the following:

1. **Regular Exercise:** Engaging in regular physical activity improves physical health and mental well-being. Aim for at least 30 minutes of moderate exercise most days.

2. **Balanced Nutrition:** A well-rounded diet fuels your body and mind.

Consider meal prepping and planning to ensure you have nutritious meals ready and make smarter food choices.

3. **Mental Well-Being:** Prioritize your mental health through mindfulness, meditation, or therapy. A clear, focused mind can enhance productivity and decision-making.

4. **Routine Check-Ups:** Preventive care is essential. Schedule regular check-ups and screenings to catch any potential health issues before they become more serious and costly.

5. **Stress Management:** High stress can take a toll on both your mental and financial health. Practice stress management techniques such as yoga, deep breathing, or enjoying hobbies.

The Financial Benefits of Good Health

Investing in your health leads to long-term financial benefits:

1. **Lower Medical Bills:** Healthy individuals typically face fewer medical expenses and emergencies.

2. **Increased Productivity:** With better health, you're likely to be more productive at work, resulting in potentially higher earnings or promotional opportunities.

3. **Long-Term Financial Security:** Good health can lead to a longer life, meaning more time to enjoy the fruits of your labor and potentially reducing the need for long-term care.

Conclusion

Prioritizing your health is an investment with far-reaching financial implications. By focusing on regular exercise, nutrition, mental well-being, routine check-ups, and stress management, you can cultivate a lifestyle that not only enhances your health but helps secure your financial future. Remember, health is indeed wealth; investing in yourself is the first step toward long-term prosperity.

Chapter 12: Lifestyle Choices: Spending Less to Live More

The Connection Between Lifestyle Choices and Wealth

The way you choose to live your life can have a powerful impact on your financial trajectory. Wealthy individuals often make strategic lifestyle choices that prioritize saving and investing while allowing them to enjoy their lives. In this chapter, we'll explore how to make lifestyle choices that enhance your happiness and financial well-being.

Minimalism: The Power of Less

Minimalism isn't just a trendy lifestyle; it's a philosophy that encourages reducing material possessions to minimize distractions and promote financial freedom. Wealthy individuals often embrace minimalism as a means to align their spending with their values.

1. **Declutter:** Evaluate your belongings and remove what you don't use or need. Selling or donating items can free up space in your home and put additional money in your pocket.

2. **Focus on Quality:** Emphasizing quality over quantity in your purchases means seeking durable, long-lasting items that provide greater value.

3. **Reduce Impulsive Purchases:** Before purchasing something, ask yourself if it aligns with your values or if it's just an

impulse buy. Delaying gratification for a few days can help you determine if you genuinely want or need the item.

Practicing Mindful Spending

Mindful spending involves being aware of where your money goes and how purchases align with your values and goals. Here's how to practice mindful spending:

1. **Create a Budget:** A budget helps you align your spending with your priorities. Take charge of your finances by tracking your expenses and setting boundaries.

2. **Prioritize Experiences Over Items:** Invest in experiences, such as travel, education, and special moments with loved ones. These tend to provide more fulfillment than material possessions.

3. **Evaluate Subscription Services:** Review your subscriptions—are they

adding value to your life? Cancel any unused services to save money.

Cutting Costs Without Sacrificing Quality

You don't have to forego quality to cut costs. Consider these strategies:

1. **Buy Generic:** For everyday items like groceries or household goods, purchasing generic brands can save you money without sacrificing quality.

2. **Utilize Loyalty Programs:** Join store loyalty or reward programs that offer savings or discounts on future purchases.

3. **DIY Projects:** Instead of hiring for small jobs, consider tackling them yourself. Whether it's simple home repairs or cooking your meals, DIY can save you money and teach you valuable skills.

Conclusion

Your lifestyle choices impact your financial health more than you might realize. By embracing minimalism, practicing mindful spending, and cutting costs wisely, you can enhance your financial situation while still enjoying life. Remember, wealth isn't solely about accumulating money; it's also about making choices that foster happiness and fulfillment.

Chapter 13: The Importance of Financial Literacy: Knowledge is Key

Understanding Financial Literacy

Financial literacy refers to the knowledge and skills necessary to make informed and effective decisions regarding personal finance. Understanding the basics of finances is crucial for building wealth and achieving financial security. This chapter will explore the key concepts of financial literacy and how to enhance your financial knowledge.

The Building Blocks of Financial Literacy

1. **Budgeting:** Understanding how to create and maintain a budget is fundamental to managing money effectively. A well-structured budget aids in tracking spending and saving goals.

2. **Saving and Investing:** Knowing the difference between saving and investing, along with how to grow your money, is essential. Saving typically involves keeping money in a secure place for future needs, while investing aims for growth through assets that may fluctuate in value.

3. **Debt Management:** Understanding how to manage and reduce debt is critical for financial success. You should know the difference between good debt (like a mortgage) and bad debt (like high-interest credit cards).

4. **Understanding Credit:** Familiarizing yourself with credit scores, reports, and how to build and maintain good credit is necessary for making significant purchases, such as a home or car.

5. **Insurance and Risk Management:** Learning about different types of insurance—such as health, life, and property—helps protect your financial well-being against unexpected events.

Resources for Financial Education

1. **Books and Blogs:** There are countless books and blogs dedicated to personal

finance. Some excellent places to start include "Rich Dad Poor Dad" by Robert Kiyosaki or blogs like "The Motley Fool" for investing tips.

2. **Online Courses:** Websites like Coursera or Udemy offer financial literacy courses. These can provide valuable education on various financial topics at your own pace.

3. **Podcasts and YouTube:** Many experts share knowledge through podcasts and YouTube channels, making it easy to learn while you're on the go. Check out podcasts like "The Dave Ramsey Show" or "ChooseFI" for informative financial discussions.

4. **Financial Advisors:** Seeking guidance from a qualified financial advisor can offer personalized insights and help you build a customized financial strategy.

Embracing Continuous Learning

Financial literacy is not a one-time endeavor; it's an ongoing process. Make it a habit to regularly educate yourself about financial matters. Follow financial news and trends to keep your knowledge fresh and relevant.

Conclusion

Financial literacy is foundational to wealth-building and managing personal finances. By understanding budgeting, saving, investing, credit management, and insurance, you can make better financial decisions that positively impact your future. Take the initiative to seek resources, educate yourself, and prioritize financial literacy.

Chapter 14: Side Hustles: Creating Additional Income Streams

The Rise of the Side Hustle

In today's gig economy, side hustles have become increasingly popular. Many wealthy individuals tap into side hustles to create additional income streams that can contribute to their financial goals. In this chapter, we'll explore the benefits of side hustles and how to find one that fits your lifestyle and skills.

Why Consider a Side Hustle?

1. **Extra Income:** The most obvious benefit of a side hustle is additional income. This extra cash can be used for savings, investments, or paying down debt.

2. **Financial Security:** Relying solely on one income source can be risky. A side

hustle provides a safety net and can be especially helpful in uncertain economic times.

3. **Pursue Passions:** A side hustle allows you to explore your passions outside your regular job. Whether it's crafting, writing, or consulting, side gigs can offer creative outlets.

4. **Skill Development:** Engaging in a side hustle can help you develop new skills and expand your network, which can benefit your primary career.

Finding the Right Side Hustle

1. **Assess Your Skills and Interests:** Think about what you enjoy doing and what skills you possess. A side hustle should be rewarding, so choose something you are passionate about or skilled in.

2. **Research Opportunities:** Consider options such as freelancing, tutoring, or becoming an online seller. Websites like Upwork, Etsy, or TaskRabbit can connect you with opportunities that align with your abilities.

3. **Leverage Your Career:** Use your current skills to find freelance work. Many professionals offer services outside their full-time jobs, such as consulting, writing, or web design.

4. **Explore Gig Economy Platforms:** Apps like Uber, Lyft, or DoorDash offer flexible opportunities to earn money on your schedule. Choose gigs that fit your lifestyle and commitments.

Balancing Time and Energy

Managing a side hustle alongside a full-time job can be challenging. Here are strategies to balance your time effectively:

1. **Set Boundaries:** Clearly define working hours for your side hustle to prevent burnout. Manage your time wisely and avoid overcommitting.

2. **Create a Schedule:** Plan your week in advance, allocating specific blocks of time for your side hustle. This organization can help you remain focused and efficient.

3. **Start Small:** If you're new to side hustles, consider starting small and gradually increasing your involvement. This approach allows you to test the waters without overwhelming yourself.

Success Stories

Consider seeking inspiration from successful side hustlers. Browse forums or social media groups where individuals share their experiences, challenges, and triumphs.

Learning from others can provide valuable insights as you develop your side hustle.

Conclusion

Side hustles can significantly contribute to your wealth-building journey. By finding opportunities that align with your skills and interests, you can generate additional income while enhancing your financial security. Embrace the side hustle culture, and start exploring options that work for you.

Chapter 15: Future Planning: Building Wealth for Generations

The Importance of Future Planning

Planning for the future is essential in securing not just your financial well-being but also that of future generations. Wealthy individuals often engage in comprehensive planning to ensure their families remain financially secure. This chapter explores the importance of future planning and actionable steps to build wealth for generations.

Setting Long-Term Goals

Establishing long-term financial goals is the first step in future planning. Consider what you want to achieve—retirement, funding education for children, or leaving a legacy. Clear goals provide direction for your financial strategies.

1. **Retirement Savings:** Start contributing to retirement accounts early to take advantage of compound interest. Assess your estimated retirement needs and adjust your savings strategies accordingly.
2. **Education Funds:** Consider setting up 529 plans or custodial accounts for

your children's education. Investing in their education can provide significant long-term benefits.

3. **Legacy Planning:** Think about the kind of legacy you want to leave behind. Estate planning allows you to decide how your assets will be distributed. Establishing a will or a trust can help ensure your wishes are honored and can minimize tax burdens.

Building an Emergency Fund

Part of future planning includes establishing a robust emergency fund. Aim to save three to six months' worth of expenses in an easily accessible account. This fund can provide financial security during unexpected situations without derailing your long-term goals.

Investing for the Future

Diversifying your investment portfolio is critical for long-term growth. Consider more aggressive investment strategies when you're younger, allowing time for growth while gradually shifting to more conservative strategies as you age.

1. **Real Estate Investments:** As discussed in previous chapters, investing in real estate can be an effective method to build wealth over time.
2. **Stock Market Investments:** Opt for a mix of individual stocks, ETFs, or mutual funds to create a balanced portfolio that aligns with your risk tolerance and goals.

Regularly Reassess Your Financial Strategies

Future planning is not a one-time effort. Regularly review your financial situation, goals, and investment strategies. Adjust your plans as necessary, accounting for changes in your income, expenses, or family dynamics.

The Power of Generosity

Consider incorporating philanthropy into your financial legacy. Wealthy individuals often focus on giving back to their communities or causes they care about. Establishing a charitable foundation or participating in local projects can create lasting impact while also teaching future generations the value of helping others.

Conclusion

Future planning is essential for achieving financial security and building wealth for generations. By setting long-term goals, investing wisely, creating an emergency fund, and regularly reassessing your strategies, you can establish a lasting financial legacy that benefits your family and community.

Embrace this vital aspect of wealth-building as you embark on your financial journey, ensuring that your efforts today lead to prosperity tomorrow.

Final Thoughts

Congratulations on completing **"Money-Saving Secrets Only the Rich Know!"** By implementing the strategies discussed in this book, you are on your way to mastering your finances, enriching your life, and potentially achieving financial freedom. Remember that the journey to wealth is not just about accumulating money; it's about making informed choices, fostering a positive mindset, and continuously striving for improvement. Your financial future is in your hands!

www.ingramcontent.com/pod-product-compliance
Lightning Source LLC
Chambersburg PA
CBHW070351230526
45471CB00006B/2520